NLP

Achieving Nlp And Life Coaching Excellence: Creating Expert-Level Success And Influence Structure

(Attain A Victorious Mindset To Attain Success In Both Professional Endeavors And Interpersonal Connections)

Anthony Owens

TABLE OF CONTENT

The Essential Components Of Neuro Linguistic Programming.. 1

What Are Metaprograms?.. 6

A Training Exercise In Thinking About Outcomes: Drawing Well-Formed Conclusions 24

Dealing With Setback 48

Pacing And Leading - Two Techniques Utilized In Neuro-Linguistic Programming (Nlp)........................ 55

The Habit Of Subconscious Consumption.................. 67

Individuals Are A Critical Factor In Attaining Any Objective Or Goal.. 77

By Altering The Stimuli Perceived By The Cerebral Cortex, We Effectively Modify Our Emotional States. 86

The Juxtaposition Of Incompetence And Expertise 99

Deciphering Indications: Non-Verbal Communication Cues In Nlp.. 102

Additional Nlp Strategies For Rethinking Negative Beliefs 117

How To Feel Motivated..131

The Essential Components Of Neuro Linguistic Programming

Values

Values pertain to the fundamental principles and beliefs that one deems highly significant and indispensable. These values are not indicative of superficial or universally applicable values. Consequently, it is imperative that you maintain utmost honesty while evaluating your values. Please consider the possibility of recording your fundamental and essential values on a sheet of paper, enabling their easy accessibility for future consultation while engaging in the techniques of Neuro Linguistic Programming.

Time

In Neuro Linguistic Programming, the concept of time pertains to the series of experiences and events encountered by an individual at distinct junctures. As an illustration, the commemorative convocation ceremony at your esteemed university serves as a profoundly unforgettable occasion, instilling within you an impassioned aspiration to pursue a career as a distinguished university professor. Alternatively, it could indicate that your inclination towards social work stems from your previous encounters with impoverished living conditions. Put differently, the passage of time will play a critical role in determining future developments. As previously mentioned, future pacing entails engaging in cognitive and affective rehearsal of the desired state or outcome.

Meta programs

Meta programs encompass a set of specialized Neuro Linguistic Programming techniques crafted to aptly anticipate and discern the individual inclinations of individuals towards other individuals, circumstances, or objects. Once you possess the ability to anticipate, perceive, and anticipate an individual's inclination regarding a matter or predicament, you can leverage that knowledge to establish or undermine rapport. Furthermore, the acquired understanding of meta programs can be effectively utilized to manipulate or convince another individual into undertaking an action they would not typically engage in. Therefore, meta programs represent sophisticated NLP techniques that necessitate ongoing familiarity among individuals who regularly employ them. Meta programs fall outside the purview of this study.

Modelling

Modelling pertains to the methodical transmission of behaviors, attitudes, and preferences from one individual to another. This is accomplished by actively emulating the qualities, conduct, mindset, and inclinations of an individual who has already achieved success in a particular pursuit. By imitating individuals who have achieved success, one can expedite the attainment of favorable outcomes as opposed to merely studying their actions verbatim. This is due to the fact that imitating or replicating the actions of a successful individual are inherently more instinctive and rational when compared to alternative methodologies.

What Are Metaprograms?

The metaprograms function as cognitive filters through which we perceive and construct our internal representations of reality. The human brain engages in extensive information processing through metaprograms, which it organizes using structures to aid in prioritization. In doing so, we can establish a strong rapport and cultivate enhanced channels of communication.

"Allow us to briefly examine each filter of the metaprograms, in order to provide you with a more comprehensive understanding of their nature:

Relocating / Drawing near

Relocating: This demographic exhibits a tendency to evade and acknowledge issues, adopting a focus primarily on undesirable aspects. "In their case, it is necessary to utilize expressions that contain a pessimistic connotation:

Failure to complete your assignments will result in a subpar academic performance."

Emerging: they are individuals who articulate through accomplishments, concerns, and ambit. They typically prioritize a positive approach, engaging in positive discussions with them.

Our objective is to increase our earnings in the current quarter.

Global / Details

On a global scale, individuals possess a broader perspective and commonly express it in the following manner:

By and large, this appears to be ...

Elaboration: As implied by their appellation, they pay meticulous attention to minor particulars; hence, they ought to be enunciated in the following manner:

In the month of May, our objective is to attain a target of 23.5% in ..."

Internal / external

Intrinsic: While engaging with them, it is imperative to center your attention on the inner aspects, relying upon your emotions and exercising self-restraint. They have a preference for making decisions, with them one engages in conversation:

The outcome is solely contingent upon your decision.

External individuals rely on and are reliant upon others, perceiving an element of external control and seeking feedback. "You are advised to communicate with them in a similar manner, roughly as follows:

We have observed that similar circumstances have resulted in favorable outcomes for others.

Past-oriented / Future-oriented

Their mindset is primarily inclined towards the past, as they have a tendency to direct their attention to prior events and favor the utilization of expressions pertaining to historical moments.

"During the previous year, in my conversation with ...".

Anticipating the future: they have a propensity to devote their attention to the forthcoming times, thus necessitating the use of language centered around future-oriented concepts.

We are pleased to announce that there will be a new project scheduled for next week."

Options / Procedures

Individuals characterized by a propensity to venture into uncharted territories and devote their attention to the act of selection. They possess an admiration for diversity, embarking upon numerous endeavors, yet their propensity to complete them is not consistently demonstrated. Words pertaining to choices must be employed in conjunction with the corresponding options.

You have the autonomy to make a decision regarding your preferences ...

Procedures encompass individuals who adhere to established regulations and specific guidelines. These individuals emblemize utmost respect for adhering to protocol, thereby necessitating the use of explicit language pertaining to unambiguous procedures.

"It is imperative that you commence the process from step 1 onwards until reaching step 9 to ...".

Proactive / Reactive

Proactive: They are individuals who derive pleasure from engaging in activities, assuming control, and taking on responsibilities. They have a strong preference for being in positions of authority. It is imperative for them to employ expressions associated with the undertaking.

It is imperative that you take immediate action ...

Proactive individuals display a tendency to defer to others for leadership, meticulously assess objectives and potential alternatives. To initiate conversation with them, employ expressions pertaining to the act of waiting: "

Kindly await the boss's response to ...".

Rapport

Establishing a strong rapport or achieving mutual tuning is imperative in order to achieve optimal effectiveness in communications. Frequently, this outcome is attained through intuitive means, necessitating an observance of the recipient's responses and a gradual exploration of discernible language patterns that evoke corresponding reactions. Not only does verbal communication hold significance, but non-verbal cues, such as body language, also wield noteworthy influence.

In order to establish rapport, it is important to possess knowledge regarding the communication patterns of individuals, including their non-verbal cues such as gestures, tone of voice, and physical posture. It pertains to establishing fortuitous correlations and contemplation, replicating while upholding due regard for the other's standpoint, in order to reflect one's own image.

When observing a couple currently in a dating relationship, one is likely to observe the phenomenon of unconsciously mirroring body positions. You may perform the experiment whilst engaged in conversation with an individual, specifically when they are discussing a topic that brings them joy. In this context, it is advised to mimic their bodily gestures and postures, followed by modifying your own behavior to exhibit the opposite. After a brief pause, proceed to replicate their gestures once again. It appears that you are engaging in rapport.

The nature of beliefs and strategies for undermining them

Beliefs encompass assessments and appraisals regarding both our own identities as well as those of others. In the field of Natural Language Processing

(NLP), generalizations that are firmly anchored in causality are deemed to be valid.

The majority of the recollections were fabricated by your mind in order to conform to your cognitions. In every given circumstance, one retains what is most significant to them.

When seeking to convince others, it is possible to encounter recollections synthesized by their cognitive processes and convictions that impede the effectiveness of your communication. It is imperative that you undermine those convictions.

When it comes to matters of faith, allow me to introduce you to Roger Bannister, an individual who established a milestone by completing a mile run in under 4 minutes. Despite the prevailing belief in the impossibility of such an accomplishment, he dedicated nine years to meticulous preparation and persistent efforts before finally achieving success. Subsequently, once he accomplished this feat, the barrier was shattered six weeks thereafter. Consequently, within the ensuing nine years, an excess of 200 individuals surpassed the established record. That belief was shattered.

A method of altering one's beliefs involves establishing a connection between severe discomfort and the existing belief, while simultaneously linking intense gratification with the new belief. One might question the degree of incredulity or irrationality associated with this belief, or inquire about its source and weigh the consequences of not eliminating it from one's life. Assign a specific designation to the sensation of pain and alter the underlying conviction associated with it.

For instance, individuals who hold the belief that "I lack the ability to dance due to my lack of coordination" will inevitably find themselves relegated to the sidelines, watching others revel in the joyous atmosphere without actively participating. Seeking mentorship in dance, enrolling in an educational institution, and confronting and overcoming the fears associated with social judgement are ways to dispel self-doubt and develop proficiency in this artistic form.

An alternative method for challenging entrenched beliefs involves presenting illustrative instances. This represents an anomaly or data point that deviates from the prevailing generalization of the observable reality. They serve as a means of challenging established beliefs, enabling the questioning of universality and facilitating a more comprehensive understanding. You employ inclusive terminology, such as "every individual, never, always, nobody," similar to the unprecedented feat accomplished by no one else before Bannister could.

The Significance of Sensory Acuity

The significance of sensory acuity (SA) cannot be overstated, as it serves as the foundation for the mastery of effective communication. Furthermore, in the realm of Natural Language Processing (NLP), Sentiment Analysis (SA) holds significant significance due to the following rationales:

- In order to develop connections with oneself and others, self-awareness is indispensable.

For individuals seeking to instigate transformations in their lives, SA is an imperative prerequisite as it equips them with the ability to decipher the indications that will steer them towards their desired objective.

- SA provides assistance to individuals in mitigating potential losses or failures before they materialize.

- Through the utilization of self-awareness, individuals are positioned favorably to discern whether they have achieved the optimal state of exceptional quality necessary to attain a goal or bring about a transformation in their lives.

A Practice to Enhance Sensory Awareness

Prior to proceeding to the subsequent phase, we kindly request that you diligently peruse each step of the exercise and execute the requisite action. Four steps are available. Upon the conclusion of the event, it will be imperative for you to possess knowledge pertaining to how comprehensive comprehension of your surroundings can result in significant and advantageous encounters for yourself.

Consider a scenario within your domestic or professional environment that evokes a certain level of unease or discontent, albeit without reaching a critical or grave magnitude. Reconstruct the event within your consciousness and envision yourself observing it as if it were being recorded by a camera, rather than merely recalling it as a mental flashback. To enhance your concentration, you may consider closing your eyes. Witness this authentic cinematic experience as it unfolds in real time while immersing yourself in the accompanying musical composition.

Please make an effort to recall the precise occurrence of this event, including your sensory and emotional experiences. (The author finds themselves in the exasperating situation of being trapped in a dense vehicular congestion.)

Break State. In the field of NLP, such conduct entails assuming a standing posture and engaging in sequential arm and leg movements to facilitate physical stimulation. Consider selecting a piece of music that you hold a great affinity for subsequent to the process of breaking state. Choose something that starkly contrasts with the emotional atmosphere evoked by the original score of the cinematic production being referenced. It is likely that your thoughts will prompt you to explore a diverse selection of musical compositions. Choose only one, please. (Indeed, the author had envisaged three musical compositions: Deep Purple's Highway Star, Queen's Don't Stop Me Now, and

Gary Numan's Cars.) The selected musical composition was Highway Star.

Please actively seek to review the footage in real-world context and immerse yourself in the role of an editing professional within a film production facility. Subsequently, during the second phase, integrate the chosen music soundtrack." Please refrain from replacing the original tone; instead, appropriately blend your audio, similar to the manner in which a movie theme is incorporated. Please view the video while ensuring that the accompanying theme music is audible.

Similarly to the second stage, enter a state of disruption. Please replay the video, omitting the theme music that was introduced in the third segment. What was the actual occurrence or event that you observed in reality?

The viewing of the video during the third stage did not invoke any adverse emotions, as observed by the author while conducting this exercise within a seminar setting, in contrast to the response experienced during the initial flashback conducted in the first stage. Nevertheless, it was revealed in the experiment that no adverse emotions were experienced during the fourth stage when the video was replayed without the accompanying audio. According to a specialist who facilitated the NLP seminar, the majority of responses to these exercises indicated a complete lack of adverse emotions during the fourth stage. There have been suggestions made that there has been a notable decrease in negative emotions. This represents the anticipated response or output generated by physical activity.

To be frank, among the initial and later stages, there existed a small subset of individuals who exhibited no discernible alteration in their emotional state. It should be noted that in the field of NLP, errors are none existent, rather they are regarded as recommendations or suggestions. This distinct response indicates a diminished level of sensory acuity compared to other participants who underwent the activity. Engaging in deliberate practice and training can greatly enhance an individual's sensory acuity, especially when utilizing Neuro-Linguistic Programming (NLP) techniques.

This exercise presents compelling evidence to support the notion that sensory information has the ability to influence an individual's emotions. By acquiring the skill to diligently observe and regulate your perception of the world through the lens of neuro-linguistic programming (NLP), you will be empowered to foster a constructive mindset, consequently enhancing the quality of your life. In instances of encountering another vexing traffic situation, this writer would habitually keep a compact disc of Highway Star within the vehicle for auditory enjoyment. However, in more recent times, subsequent to the author's enhanced sensory acuity achieved through the utilization of NLP, the task merely involves the cognitive recollection of the music without the actual auditory perception. Another fundamental assumption in the field of natural language processing is the recognition of the interconnectedness between the physical and mental aspects, highlighting the significance of this aspect.

Outcome Thinking

Outcome-oriented thinking involves directing our mental faculties towards making progress in life rather than fixating on the challenging circumstances that require change. As a fundamental element of Natural Language Processing (NLP), the contemplation of outcomes strives for an equitable position that will foster mutual benefit in order to accomplish a specific goal - a transformative change in one's life. An individual's understanding of the nuances of thought will impact their capacity to steer their actions towards achieving transformative outcomes. Your concept has a direct impact on the outcome of your endeavors.

In order to achieve the desired outcomes, the adoption of an outcome-focused mindset entails a systematic approach to refining and fine-tuning objectives or targets. Contemplating the outcomes enhances the likelihood of attaining the intended enhancement, as engaging in the process of refining one's strategies and approaches fosters a "programming" of the mind to believe in the comprehensive feasibility of the system and the actualization of the desired outcome.

A Training Exercise In Thinking About Outcomes: Drawing Well-Formed Conclusions

In order to conceive coherent findings, several methodologies are employed. This framework was established in 2005, drawing inspiration from the principles articulated by Peter McNab. As an outcome of this exercise, think of something you want to change in your life. Approach this task with utmost dedication, as it marks the inaugural phase of your pursuit to discover newfound meaning in your life. Record the inquiries in a journal or notebook, and proceed to attend to them.

• In what aspect of your life would you like to make alterations? Kindly express your response in an affirmative manner. It is advisable to afford you, at the very least, partial control over this outcome.

• Regarding this transition in your life, please indicate where, when, and in whose presence you desire it to occur.

- Which metrics have successfully attained the desired outcome?
- Is your current behavior in alignment with the desired outcome or intended transformation? If your priorities do not align with this behavior, what are the potential consequences of altering it?
- Could other factors in your life influence the outcome you desire?
- In which particular domains or under which specific circumstances would you be inclined to abstain from pursuing the intended outcome?
- Are there any impediments that you perceive, if any, that hinder your current ability to experience the desired outcome? Do you possess any supplementary resources required?
- How are you preparing to achieve the result you want? When would you put your strategy into action to get the result?

The responses provided to the inquiries may necessitate periodic evaluation, with the exclusion of the final outcome. In order to enhance the probability of attaining your intended outcome, it is imperative that you carefully improve your responses to these inquiries and subsequently revise them. The aforementioned exercise embodies the procedure of generating an outcome that is structurally sound, serving as the focal point or primary goal of pondering over repercussions. In order to attain the desired outcome, individuals should diligently direct their endeavors, particularly in the realms of interpersonal connections, perceptual sensitivity, and adaptive comportment.

Versatility

Behavioral versatility or general versatility is considered as the fourth pillar of NLP. The core concept underlying behavioral adaptability entails guiding oneself towards the exploration of alternative ways of functioning when the existing approach proves ineffective in attaining the intended outcome. Achieving success in the field of NLP is contingent upon one's ability to exhibit adaptability in executing actions that facilitate the attainment of desired outcomes. In the realm of natural language processing (NLP) as applied to personal growth, it is imperative to possess adaptability, as it enables one to modify their actions in order to elicit a particular response from others or attain the desired transformation within oneself.

The malleability of conduct is contingent upon established patterns of behavior. If the disruption of habits is attainable, it follows that the establishment of habits is also within reach. By engaging in thorough preparation and diligent practice, one can successfully achieve an enhanced ability to adapt and exhibit behavioral versatility. John Grinder, one of the pioneers of Neuro-Linguistic Programming (NLP), proposed that individuals engage in a nightly practice of introspection, carefully analyzing the day's occurrences and deliberately devising a minimum of three alternative approaches or responses to each specific situation encountered. This book further elaborates upon the guidance provided by Grinder in the following manner:

Record distinct events or circumstances for each day within a diary, journal, or notepad. For optimal categorization and retrieval, an electronic system for organizing files is highly recommended.

Please classify these examples according to their respective outcomes, distinguishing those that have yielded positive versus negative results.

- Please document your response to the given situation and classify the ones that were successful and the ones that were not.
- Generate a minimum of three alternative responses for each case and make a conscious effort to memorize these alternatives.
- In order to ascertain their consistent functioning, it is advisable to replicate your responses to situations that yield positive outcomes.
- Reap the advantages of the feedback you have received concerning unfavorable situations. In an analogous situation, should a similar unfavorable outcome arise in the future, it is advisable to employ one of the

alternative courses of action you have prepared as a response.

• Conduct a file organization and performance evaluation after a span of one month. Incorporate practices that have consistently demonstrated success under comparable conditions. You would be astonished by the impact that possessing behavioral adaptability can have on bolstering one's personal growth and enhancing overall happiness.

Let us reflect on those neural pathways. The human brain contains a vast assemblage of neurons numbering in the billions, which are interconnected through a staggering amount of connections in the trillions. The formation of our memories occurs as a result of the boundless neural connections within our minds, and our capacity to retrieve information stems from these neural connections. When an neural connection is established in our brain, it generates a pathway or conduit through which the identical piece of information can consistently traverse whenever the corresponding thought is contemplated. This is the process by which cognitive patterns can be formed. When one becomes accustomed to employing consistent cognitive patterns and procedures, one reinforces those neural pathways, thereby augmenting their accessibility and establishing a more profound and ingrained integration within one's brain function.

When we cultivate routines, regardless of their positive or negative nature, we are engaging in the same cognitive process, even if it operates on a subconscious level. Numerous habits indeed manifest as unconscious cognitive patterns. When the same cognitive process is repeatedly performed throughout the day, frequently over the course of a week, and persistently over the span of a year, it will consistently enhance and intensify the neural pathway linked to that particular pattern of thought.

Now, let us proceed to illustrate this through an example. Whenever an error occurs during your piano practice, you mentally label it as "stupid." Consequently, your brain establishes a neural pathway and association between playing the piano and the sensation of inadequacy or foolishness. By persisting in your practice and experiencing errors, you inadvertently perpetuate the notion of incompetence associated with making mistakes during the process of learning the piano. Over time, as you continue to engage in deliberate practice, the occurrence of errors tends to increase due to the ingrained tendency of your mind to perceive any stumbling as incompetence or foolishness. As this sentiment intensifies, there is a noticeable decline in your enthusiasm towards playing the piano, as it evokes feelings of inadequacy. Consequently, you prefer engaging in activities that do not elicit such emotions.

Within a brief timeframe, your cognitive faculties exhibited the capacity to establish a correlation between acquiring piano skills and experiencing a sense of intellectual inadequacy, thereby leading you to cease playing due to a preference for avoiding such negative emotions. What was the rationale behind your establishment of that connection? Why did you categorize your error as foolish? In all probability, due to an affiliation or correlation with another entity, an alternative mental framework, or an acquired habit. It could have originated from a stringent instructor whose insistence on perfection led to your self-doubt regarding your capabilities. It is possible that this mindset may have originated from a preceding life experience that imparted upon you the notion that committing errors is not tolerable.

Irrespective of the primary underlying factor, it manifests in all the neural pathways within the mind, and with sufficient repetition, can evolve into a cognitive framework that permeates our self-perception.

Our understanding is fundamentally shaped by the connections we draw between our existing knowledge, personal encounters, and ongoing acquisition of new information. The totality of our encounters can be predicated on the connections and associations forged within our cognitive faculties. That takes us back to the concept of subjective reality that you read about earlier.

Given your propensity for making connections and associations in your mind, do you not believe that you have the ability to transform any negative thoughts into ones that are more positive in nature? One should bear in mind that the mind possesses a malleable nature, exhibiting flexibility and the potential for transformation.

Dream Programming

The act of sleeping provides an opportune moment to entrust and contemplate problems to one's higher self. Envision issuing instructions to both components of yourself regarding any matter prior to retiring for the night. Consider yourself as the proprietor of a corporate enterprise, whereby you stipulate that upon your return (upon awakening in the morning), they are expected to furnish you with the utmost optimal resolution. Be mindful of that intent as you drift off to sleep. Subsequently, take a moment the following day to engage in the practice of recording any concepts or thoughts that may have been conceived.

Merely a Figurative Illusion

This is simply an instance of figurative language. A useful hallucination. However, the act of envisioning two distinct components with whom you can engage in conversation, as though they exist independently from you, can assist in fostering a more impartial perspective on your concerns. One should not be astonished if, upon continued experimentation with these methods, they start yielding exceedingly innovative solutions.

Try Ideas Slowly

Another frequently observed misstep in the execution of this exercise involves approaching it as a panacea for significant issues. Significant challenges seldom find quick and simplistic resolutions. Regard this as an opportunity to unveil additional imaginative prospects for resolution. Display a willingness to explore these proposed solutions, while regarding them as prospective resolutions. Take a gradual approach and observe the outcomes. Subsequently, allow the two factions to engage in a comprehensive dialogue pertaining to the outcomes and subsequently determine the subsequent course of action.

Compulsion Blow Out

This pattern possesses significant potency and should exclusively be applied in cases of urgency. Indeed, while I wouldn't necessarily classify these situations as emergencies, they do pertain to tasks that one strongly desires to avoid at all costs. This pattern, however, offers an effective solution to handle such circumstances. This can be likened to the antithesis of an anchor. An anchor refers to the process of establishing a connection between an internal physiological response and an external response. A significant number of these patterns and ideas incorporate the concept of anchoring. Each time the swish pattern is implemented, an alteration is elicited in one's internal reaction to an external stimulus. On a macroscopic level, the vast majority of our emotions arise as reactions to stimuli originating from external occurrences or internal recollections. The primary objective of NLP is to strategically transition a significant portion of our thoughts, including the thoughts that influence our thinking patterns, from operating automatically to being consciously directed. Primarily, we dissect innate processes, analyze them, and subsequently endeavor to reshape our perspectives to encompass alternative approaches. In most cases, this entails ascribing a heightened sense of resourcefulness or a range of emotions to a concept or an externally manifested action. We desire to experience joy and contentment upon encountering canines within the park. We aspire to enhance our sense of resourcefulness in moments of conflict. We want to feel more control of our emotions in more situations. Contrarily, this pattern exhibits an inverse effect.

Behavior Removal Pattern

This is intended for a task or obligation that you no longer wish to continue. This is typically correlated with the consumption of particular detrimental food items. It is advised against utilizing this substance for alcohol or drugs (including tobacco) due to the multitude of variables associated with them. This pattern is intended for a particular culinary item or a specific conduct that one wishes to cease. Please ensure that you are certain in your decision to cease this behavior, as this method operates on the premise that your intention is to contemplate the most dreadful scenario imaginable and deliberately link that scenario to the particular behavior you wish to refrain from consuming.

Donuts

Let us illustrate this with donuts. However, the food or behavior in consideration should ideally lack any concealed variables and exhibit a reasonable level of certainty. Alcohol, drugs, and excessive consumption of food are intricately linked to more profound and intricate concerns. However, in the event that there is a singular food item that you earnestly desire did not exist, given that you consistently adhere to a nutritious diet, this is the observed trend. For the purposes of illustration, we shall employ donuts as our exemplar. In the given illustration, were the concept of donuts to be eradicated from collective human recollection, we would endure without any detriment. Rest assured, acquiring knowledge about this subject matter will not incite any disdain towards donuts. This pattern requires an equal amount of concentration, effort, and consistency as the others.

Step One

Ascertain the specific food item or behavioral pattern that you intend to eradicate. We shall utilize a chocolate donut infused with a luscious cream filling.

Step Two

This is the repulsive segment. This is the moment when you formulate the most repulsive notion that your mind can conceive. For the sake of our requirements, let's utilize the term 'human emesis.' And not by a relative, but by an unfamiliar individual. Somehow, allow for the manifestation of a pleasantly heated receptacle containing regurgitated matter expelled by the human body.

Step Three

Glide effortlessly between the two individuals, akin to the motion observed in the swish pattern. In the swish pattern, the initial step entails commencing with the unpleasant feeling, as you subsequently replace it with a more positive one. Once the image becomes perceptible, eliciting the initial negative emotions, you intentionally redirect your cognitive processes towards the positive image and corresponding positive emotions. By repeatedly engaging in this practice, the photo that initially evoked negative emotions (as illustrated in the previous scenario with the dog in the park inducing fear) will gradually elicit positive emotions (in this case, social confidence). The procedure remains unchanged. With the exception that one commences by disposing of the item in question (the donut) and concludes by confronting the repulsive substance (the bowl of vomit). You will be required to repeat this process multiple times until the new anchor is securely established. That whenever you see a chocolate cream filled donut, you automatically imagine slurping up a nice warm bowl of human vomit.

Conscious Practice

This approach is significantly more straightforward compared to the alternative method, as our cognitive processes tend to prioritize caution over risk. This is equally effective when applied to culinary matters. If you can get an actual item that you'd like to quit, like an actual chocolate donut, it will be helpful. Direct your attention to the donut, then proceed to firmly shut your eyes and envision the most repulsive imagery within your mind. Exert a deliberate effort to immerse your mind in the utmost realistic and intricately constructed portrayal possible. Observe, perceive, savor (including taste), and discern all aspects. Experience the auditory sensations that would be reminiscent of consuming a substantial serving of an unappetizing substance. If you happen to be in a professional setting, and you happen to come across a tray of chocolate donuts generously filled with cream, kindly pause for a brief moment to envision indulging in an alternative experience involving a less appetizing substance.

Behaviors That Pose a Slightly Greater Challenge

Managing this task becomes effortless through the act of consuming. By exerting intentional exertions and employing a modicum of innovative imagination, one can readily quell any inclination to consume undesirable food. But what about behaviors? The process remains consistent. Envision the conduct you wish to cease. Suppose you have the intention of discontinuing the habit of pressing the snooze button on your alarm clock. This task will require a certain degree of ingenuity. We will have to envision ourselves in bed once the alarm goes off. One possible approach would be to consider envisioning a scenario where, precisely one minute following the sounding of the alarm, your bed becomes occupied by an assortment of serpents, gastropods, and gelatinous sea creatures. Please be mindful that you will need to exert effort in mentally envisioning yourself lying in bed while being encircled by reptiles, aquatic creatures, and gastropods. You will need to construct a temporal barrier that spans both preceding and subsequent moments to coincide with the activation of your alarm. Prior to the sounding of your alarm, your bed serves as a secure haven of coziness and security. However, once the alarm is triggered, one has a limited duration of one minute prior to its transformation into a habitat containing jellyfish, snails, and snakes. You may choose to await the sounding of your alarm and subsequently exert effort to envision a gradual metamorphosis of your bed. Alternatively, consider the scenario where a receptacle containing spiders is situated near the foot of your bed, and the alarm causes said receptacle to become accessible. Upon the moment your alarm sounds, envision the actuation of the box, accompanied by the commencement of the spiders' ascent along the exterior of your sleeping apparatus, as they make their way towards your lower extremities. Exercise great caution in ensuring that you establish a robust linkage between the alarm system and the lock mechanism on the box. Otherwise, you may experience distressing dreams.

Exercise Prudent Deliberation Prior to Associating with Adverse Imagery

Similar to the donuts, it is important to carefully consider the behavior that is being eradicated through this procedure. Proceed ahead only if you possess full assurance that all other alternatives have been exhausted. It would be prudent to consider reserving this technique as a final option. Indulging in chocolate donuts on certain occasions is quite enjoyable, after all. However, the mere realization that any food or behavior can be linked to the most dreadful concept imaginable might serve as sufficient impetus for individuals to seek alternative methods to gradually modify their conduct.

Dealing With Setback

To what extent is one's day susceptible to being disrupted or compromised? What factors contribute to the potential for someone to negatively impact your day and evoke feelings of distress? And what is the frequency at which you allow this to occur in your daily routine?

Maintaining one's sense of perspective can prove challenging during adverse circumstances. In an instant, everything may appear to be proceeding smoothly and one's day may seem to be proceeding in an ordinary manner. However, unforeseen challenges may arise, and when they do, a sense of heaviness may loom over an individual, persisting throughout the entirety of their day. You are unlikely to encounter any positive experiences during the course of your day, allowing the oppressive gloom to envelop your being.

Make a Move!

By allowing oneself to be affected by someone else's conduct, one places oneself in a vulnerable position to potentially fall victim to negative emotions. Given that their actions elicit a preexisting emotional response within you, you subsequently make a subconscious determination that they are the cause of your distress.

However, the reality is that they are not the cause of your negative emotions; rather, it is your disregarded anchor that is the primary issue, not their conduct.

Procedures for Restoring Perceptive Abilities via Neuro-Linguistic Programming (NLP)

Step 1: Pre-establish an alternate anchor or idea beforehand

It is advisable to establish an alternative anchor or mindset for a specific type of scenario. In the context of your professional responsibilities, it may be necessary to maintain a separate device for work-related tasks, in addition to having distinct devices for personal matters, social engagements, and other purposes. Certainly, it is possible for you to have a distinct dwelling tailored to accommodate your family's needs. However, the dynamics of your domestic circumstances present additional complexities.

Suppose you are establishing an alternative anchor that can be utilized in situations involving customer interactions. Envision all the facets that you find appealing in your occupation - the prospects for growth, the demanding nature, the financial remuneration, the pleasant clientele, and additional aspects. Compile a comprehensive enumeration of all of them on a sheet of paper. Now, consider an individualized scenario for each of them: reflect upon a moment when you experienced a stimulating sense of delight, engaging in a conversation with your employer regarding prospective avenues, contemplating the financial gains accrued in your bank account, or recalling a memorable interaction with a satisfied customer, among other instances.

Make an effort to recollect impactful memories characterized by positivity, aiming to substitute the current thoughts that have impeded the progress of your day.

Proceed to strengthen this by contemplating it on a daily basis.

Devise a substitute anchor for yourself on multiple occasions throughout the day. And execute the task in whatever manner that is most suitable to your personal preferences. Conceive of those thoughts within your mind. Please accomplish the task by drawing upon the emotions evoked by your recollections. Achieve this by employing auditory stimuli through the attentive engagement with the musical score accompanying each and every reminiscence within your repertoire.

The crucial aspect lies in ensuring that it elicits a profound emotional response regardless of the method employed.

Step 3: Employ it immediately during circumstances that disturb your demeanor.

On subsequent occasions when someone attempts to influence your demeanor, there are two courses of action available to address the situation.

The initial step entails altering your physical circumstance. Please rise from your current position, engage in physical movement by taking a stroll, consume a couple of glasses of water, alleviate the sensation through deep and deliberate breaths. By implementing these actions, you will disrupt the influence of anchoring.

Enliven your Replacement Anchor via auditory, visual, or sensory stimuli.

Step 4: Adapt your thinking to better align with the context

If you have completed all three initial steps without any success or if you sense that they are insufficient, it indicates that you should seek a more robust alternative anchor or pathway. Therefore, it is advisable to engage in positive thinking and cultivate the ability to readily embrace uplifting thoughts, as doing so will encourage the experience of heightened feelings of satisfaction and contentment.

Pacing And Leading - Two Techniques Utilized In Neuro-Linguistic Programming (Nlp)

There exist multiple methodologies in neurolinguistic programming that facilitate establishing a connection with another individual. This interpersonal connection, alternatively referred to as rapport or pacing, can be likened to a conduit of communication. "Pacing" refers to a reflective approach wherein the conversational participant, akin to a coach, adapts to the counterpart and emulates their communication style. The coach establishes a mirrored reflection wherein they provide understated feedback to demonstrate alignment with the interlocutor.

Once a foundation of trust has been established through this process, the coach transitions into a state of "leading". By doing so, the individual assumes the role of the conversation's initiator. This method may also be employed to exert influence over the other individual and prompt specific behavioral responses. Nevertheless, this should not serve as the foundation for neuro-linguistic programming. Utilizing leadership should instead be employed to foster alternative viewpoints on the individual's concerns and to explore potential resolutions.

Formats within the realm of neurolinguistic programming constitute various methodologies or strategies. There does not exist a fundamental theorem grounded in scientific theory. There are no established methods either. Neuro-linguistic programming represents a conglomeration of diverse strategies designed to facilitate cognitive transformation. The communication and intervention options are referred to as "formats" and encompass meticulously defined sequences of actions and tools that are utilized to effectuate positive change.

All individuals utilizing NLP possess a comprehensive toolkit at their disposal. One may come across both shared and distinct formats, yet they share a common attribute. They are rooted in the internal capabilities that aid in the resolution of an individual's specific problem. They have the capability to address and resolve issues originating from the past. The primary emphasis is consistently directed towards progressive transformation. Neuro-linguistic programming possesses the capability to reframe and recontextualize unfavorable experiences, transforming them into constructive encounters that can influence future behaviors. Consequently, the allocation of resources becomes imperative in order to effectively address and surmount challenges, obstacles, disturbances, or anxieties.

In order for the endeavor to attain success, deliberate constructs of discussion and definitive courses of action are established as a foundation. The coach's orientation and demeanor should align with the principles of humanistic ethics and values. This is primarily due to the fact that neuro-linguistic programming occasionally incorporates elements of a mild trance or hypnosis state. This facilitates the transfer of positive perceptions into the realm of cognitive awareness.

One of the most renowned methodologies within the realm of neuro-linguistic programming pertains to "reframing," wherein a particular situation is subject to reinterpretation, thereby instilling it with a novel significance. This outcome is accomplished by situating it within a novel framework. Alternative formats employ techniques such as visualization or autosuggestion. The practice of autosuggestion entails employing the repetition of positive affirmations alongside the establishment of constructive thought patterns. In the realm of visualization, one focuses mental faculties towards the prospective achievements, conjuring a vivid mental representation that embodies the desired state of mind upon accomplishing the objective.

Each incarnation of neuro-linguistic programming has been intricately devised to enable the human consciousness to disentangle itself from negative behavioral patterns and thought processes, while concurrently facilitating the establishment of new, affirmative ones. The core significance possesses greater behavioral adaptability as it provides a broader range of possibilities for one's own conduct. As a result, it engenders greater liberty and enhances the overall standard of living. Consequently, it is imperative that the ethical principles upheld by both the individual and the coach align to ensure that the interventions proceed towards the intended course.

5. Circle of Excellence

The Circle of Excellence provides a remarkable opportunity to leverage your innate strengths and positive attributes in order to enhance various facets of your life. This approach enables individuals to achieve complete autonomy over their emotional states, facilitating the ability to modify their behavior in the intended fashion. Given that optimal outcomes are unattainable without being in an appropriate emotional state, it is imperative that you make a transformative shift in your current disposition.

Your emotional condition pertains to your current emotional experience. In the event that you experience adverse emotional states or feelings of vulnerability, it is highly probable that you lack mastery over your emotions and are unable to fully exploit your capabilities.

In order to cultivate a robust emotional state, it is imperative to exercise dominion over the realm of the subconscious mind, and the utilization of the circle of excellence technique assists in achieving this objective.

Effective Strategies for Implementing the Circle of Excellence Technique in Your Practice

Presented below is the methodology for effectively honing your skills in this potent NLP technique.

1. Please kindly close your eyes and envision drawing a large circle within your mind. Visualize the circular shape positioned directly in front of you on the surface, with dimensions sufficient for allowing you to easily occupy its space by stepping into it. Should you desire,

you are welcome to trace a circular shape on the ground using a piece of chalk as well.

2. Envision the multitude of positive attributes that you possess. Extract all of your strengths, previous achievements, and optimism, and transfer them into the hypothetical perimeter. This signifies your sphere of utmost distinction. It is possible to assign specific hues to distinctive attributes. For example, courage may take on the appearance of whiteness, while peacefulness may manifest as a shade of green, and so forth.

3. After creating a sphere of exceptional aptitude and positivity, proceed to enter it.

4. Inhale deeply and begin to perceive the diverse positive frequencies that emanate from within that enclosed perimeter. Embrace the notion that the

positive qualities encapsulated within the confines of the circle are permeating your being, leading to a transformation into a remarkable individual. Savor this sensation and indulge in it for however long you desire. If you so desire, you have the option to associate this sensation with a specific action, similar to the manner in which you employed the 'new behavior generator' approach.

5. Please ensure your eyes are open and proceed to rehearse the specific movement you have just associated with your zone of optimal performance. Envision the act of retrieving your emblem of exceptional achievement and conveniently placing it within the confines of your trouser or outer garment pocket.

Whenever you experience a sense of melancholy, retrieve that symbol of exceptional capabilities and employ it to experience an elevated state of being. Utilize your anchor to initiate the activation of that sphere of exceptional ability and experience the force it imparts upon you. With the support of your esteemed network, you will effortlessly cultivate a sense of enthusiasm towards your professional endeavors, hasten task completion, and diligently pursue your aspirations to expedite the attainment of success.

Utilize this methodology whenever you experience uncertainty, discontent, or strain, and you will effectively surmount your deficiencies and vulnerable emotional state.

The 'Picture Frame' method is an additional NLP technique which can aid individuals in addressing a state of emotional weakness and negativity, by effectively reframing distressing occurrences.

The Habit Of Subconscious Consumption

What did you have for breakfast this morning? Did you partake in your customary selection? Does your customary French toast come with a generous drizzle of maple syrup, paired with two fried eggs alongside, or possibly a serving of cereal? Do you partake in breakfast on a daily basis? Have you taken the time to assess your hunger and evaluate the specific nutritional requirements of your body prior to consuming your morning meal? Alternatively, did you happen to proceed with the actions of preparing and consuming breakfast merely out of a sense of urgency, without giving significant thought to the process?

"The Practice of Engaging in Inattentive Eating:

Individuals commonly consume a significant portion of their snacks and meals without being fully aware or mindful of their actions. Do you consume all the food you have served yourself during dinner? Alternatively, do you opt for second servings due to it being a habitual practice for you? Do you have a tendency to indulge in snacking while viewing the afternoon news?

- Impact of these Habits on Individuals: It is a well-known reality that each individual possesses eating habits. The lamentable aspect and consequence of this phenomenon is that mindless eating tends to result in choices that are detrimental to one's health and ultimately contribute to weight gain, an outcome that is undesirable to us.

Research indicates that a significant number of individuals in the American population engage in the habit of viewing television programs while dining, frequently neglecting the practice of having structured and seated meals. Additionally, a portion of individuals consume food during their commute to the workplace.

- Multitasking while eating is ineffective: Observe the streets of any bustling metropolis, and one will encounter numerous individuals partaking in meals while in transit. When individuals consume food while simultaneously engaging in another task, their attention is diverted from the act of eating, resulting in a potential lack of awareness regarding the quantity of food being ingested. Consequently, this may contribute to an increased likelihood of overeating. Furthermore, the act of engaging in multiple tasks simultaneously or consuming meals on the move is detrimental to the inherent physiological process of digestion in your body. Failure to chew your food thoroughly will result in weight gain and an overwhelmed digestive system.

NLP ANCHOR TECHNIQUE

I am confident that you have completed the preceding exercise, and we will now progress to an exceptionally potent NLP technique known as anchoring. We will now proceed with the creation of an anchor in this exercise. Anchor is a trigger. This method facilitates the cultivation of enhanced self-assurance in a range of contexts, including job interviews, public speaking engagements, professional presentations, stage performances, social encounters, and even interactions with individuals of the opposite gender. I would like to ensure that, during the execution of this exercise, you are in a solitary environment without any disruptions. This exercise is estimated to require approximately 10 to 15 minutes of your time. Please locate a suitable position where you can sit comfortably, ensuring to close your eyes, take several deep breaths, and allow your entire body and mind to unwind. Consider a moment from your personal history wherein you experienced a profound sense of self-assurance. At any point in your personal history, engaging in discussions with acquaintances, within your professional environment, you executed a task with exceptional proficiency, instilling within you a profound sense of assurance. Please observe the visual stimuli that were present, audibly perceive the sounds that were audible, and emotionally experience the sensations that were felt during that particular moment, as if it were transpiring in the present time. Enhance and magnify this marvelous sensation. And take note of the visual impressions that arise during that moment, the mental images that manifest. I kindly request that you increase the size of these pictures and enhance the color, making it more vibrant, striking, and pronounced. Do you recall if there was a need to increase the volume in that particular recollection of yours? Enlarge the image and bring it into closer proximity. If one observes oneself in the depiction, this indicates a state of association, whereas perceiving oneself from a distance implies a state of dissociation.

One might perceive a sense of immersion, as if figuratively entering and becoming a part of the depicted scene, effectively blending with its elements and essence. That is fully associated. Indulge in that moment once again. Observe how positively you are currently experiencing. Please take note of your considerable level of control, confidence, and willingness to partake in this delightful sensation depicted in the image. Please take note of the location within your body where this exquisite sensation is experienced. Identify the inner state of confidence and trace its manifestation. Notice where it is? Identify and instigate a more rapid rotation of those emotions. Permit them to propagate throughout your entire being, ascending from the crown of your head to the extremities of your toes.

Experience the remarkable sensation gradually circulating throughout your physique, progressively enhancing your senses with an increasing sense of vitality. Continue executing these steps until you perceive a significant amplification of that euphoric sensation. As the intensity of the sensation increases progressively, endeavor to form a manual stimulus by configuring a trigger using the thumb and middle finger of your dominant hand. Proceed by applying pressure and constricting them firmly, thus encapsulating all the positive emotions garnered. Maintain this state for a brief moment, and subsequently release the tension in a relaxed manner. Cease activation of the trigger mechanism and proceed to open your eyes, attentively observe your surroundings, reorient yourself within your immediate environment, and take notice of the notable sense of well-being you are experiencing. Now, in order to experience the same remarkable and potent sensation, simply apply gentle pressure to your thumb and middle finger of your dominant hand. Almost instantaneously, you will notice the resurfacing of that identical sense of assurance permeating your entire being - both physically and mentally. Now, you will possess a tool that can instill confidence in you, enabling you to summon it effortlessly, whenever and wherever you desire. This resource will be readily accessible at your fingertips. As an assignment, please document three instances in which you experienced a high level of confidence. Afterwards, revisit the steps once more to recreate the same response using the identical stimulus on the corresponding hand. Now, please take note that an additional action may be incorporated:

upon pinching your thumb and finger together, it is advisable to internally affirm the phrase, 'I possess a sense of self-assurance.' Immediately, this term also serves as a catalyst for you. With each declaration of self-assurance, a profound sense of assurance will permeate your entire being.

Now, during moments of reflection, should any further instances arise in which you experienced a sense of assurance, kindly close your eyes, inhale deeply, embrace the sensation, and generate an equivalent stimulus. Engaging in such action fortifies your trigger significantly, ultimately culminating in your confidence trigger being effectively activated. The greater frequency of utilization corresponds to an increase in its potency. Please proceed to repeat this exercise once more, after which we can transition to the subsequent lesson, where I will introduce the upcoming technique.

Individuals Are A Critical Factor In Attaining Any Objective Or Goal.

The meaning:

At times, one may observe the accomplishment of a desired aspiration in someone else, leading to the emergence of envy and a sense of personal limitation in terms of achieving remarkable feats.

It is likely that you have encountered this previously, however, permit me to suggest that if an individual were to attain a certain accomplishment, it is within your capabilities to do the same.

Occasionally, individuals hinder their own progress by harboring the belief that they are unworthy of certain achievements or opportunities. This self-deprecating mindset materializes in the subconscious, leading to an ingrained perception that success or desired outcomes are unattainable for them.

It is imperative to cultivate the belief that one can attain or acquire what others have accomplished or possess.

The recommended course of action:

It is imperative that you understand that all goals are within reach when one commits wholeheartedly. Refrain from comparing oneself to individuals who have achieved success, rather focus on cultivating one's own achievements and impact.

The primary approach to accomplishing anything entails possessing or cultivating the aptitude to attain or possess one's desired outcomes, followed by devising a strategic plan that outlines the means by which one intends to accomplish these objectives, all the while maintaining a resolute determination to embark on a path towards achievement.

I would like to offer you some guidance in order to assist you in attaining your goals. However, I regret to inform you that this guidance has the potential to be detrimental, particularly if you possess a substantial ego.

One might constantly strive for the accomplishments and aspirations pursued by others, inadvertently neglecting the abundant blessings present in their own life. Furthermore, a drawback of this presumption is that you may find yourself pursuing objectives that do not align with your own values and will not ultimately bring you contentment. For instance, you aspire to pursue a career in medicine merely due to the fact that your cousin has chosen this profession, or solely because your parents have expressed their desire for you to follow the same path. Exercise caution when discerning the objectives you aspire to accomplish within your lifetime.

"The advantages that you will receive:

Cease your comparison of self to others, for such comparisons are known to perpetuate feelings of perpetual emptiness and neediness. Through the process of comparison, one can never attain true happiness as it perpetuates a constant sense of lacking in one's life.

Envy shall not arise within your existence, as you will undoubtedly refrain from making comparisons with others and discern precisely what you desire in your life through the cultivation of your fundamental principles. And that is precisely what will guide you towards attaining your own success, independent of the aspirations or accomplishments of others.

Assumption 6: All operations ought to facilitate individual advancement.

The meaning:

There are numerous processes imparted in self-help or any given domain that prove to be of little significance. Undoubtedly, you may be acquainted with a subset of individuals commonly referred to as "fake gurus" who feign expertise in addressing your predicament. However, their claims merely consist of tips they themselves may have never attempted, ultimately driven by the intention to promote their own merchandise.

All endeavors undertaken throughout one's lifetime should serve to facilitate personal development. The reading material in question should effectively foster your personal development; in the event that it fails to do so, assuming no proactive measures are taken, the significance of the book becomes negligible.

The recommended course of action:

All procedures that you are going to acquire and engage in must facilitate individual development. As a consequence, it is imperative that you familiarize yourself with the information acquired, as it will facilitate your subsequent exercise and enhance personal growth.

Exercise utmost scrutiny in selecting both your sources of knowledge and the individuals from whom you seek guidance. As these words of counsel originate from an improper source, heeding them will inevitably lead to your downfall.

Furthermore, for individuals engaged in the process of acquiring knowledge, there exists a deep appreciation for personal growth and development. This is demonstrated through endeavors such as indulging in literature, enrolling in educational programs, seeking guidance from experienced mentors, and so forth. Take action. The acquisition of information holds no value unless it is accompanied by subsequent action.

Examine your patterns and actions that comprise your daily life. Do they foster your personal development? If this is not the case, it is prudent for you to consider making a change.

As you may be aware, your daily actions define your being. Your current patterns of behavior will shape your identity.

Please provide a detailed account of your daily activities and I will endeavor to make an informed projection of your future state.

For instance, should you cultivate the practice of engaging in reading at present, you would naturally acquire knowledge and exhibit high intelligence. Engaging in regular physical activity is conducive to achieving and maintaining optimal health and physical fitness...

The advantages that you will receive:

By selecting the methodologies that foster personal development, one will evolve into an individual who possesses daily clarity and efficiency in their actions. That implies that you shall attain wisdom.

By selecting the appropriate methods, you will attain mastery over your existence. One possesses the knowledge on how to adeptly maneuver through life and achieve prosperity contingent upon the selection of appropriate methodologies.

Through these experiences, you will ultimately attain self-improvement to reach your highest potential. Through the implementation and selection of effective methodologies that foster individual development, one ensures the cultivation of positive behaviors, resulting in the realization of one's fullest potential.

By Altering The Stimuli Perceived By The Cerebral Cortex, We Effectively Modify Our Emotional States.

Perhaps you hold the belief that the adverse emotions you have encountered in the past are immutable and destined to endure indefinitely? One must not overlook the factors that have led to their occurrence, as they possess significant intensity. Perhaps you are unable to fathom the prospect of leading a life devoid of these detrimental emotions?

Please be aware that it is entirely within your discretion to perceive these emotions as intense and the events responsible for them as substantial. This image exemplifies the world in which you have elected to reside.

Do you perceive this particular configuration of events and circumstances as the exclusive possibility? However, it is possible to alter this context. And it is imperative to recognize that alternative options exist. You have the ability to develop a new perspective on the same matter. To accomplish this, a genuine aspiration for transformation is all that is required. Moreover, it becomes evident that the responsibility for initiating these changes lies solely within your control, as the interpretation of events ultimately rests within your unique perspective. The construction of your worldview rests solely in your hands. If one were to initiate its construction, they would be exerting their influence and effecting its alteration.

You are already aware of the methodology for constructing a representation of the world. It is generated through the use of visual, auditory, and kinesthetic stimuli.

Initially, these signals are conveyed to the brain. The brain processes them. Subsequently, the emergence of emotions occurs only subsequent to this; and thereafter, conclusions and beliefs are fashioned solely subsequent to the arising of emotions.

For instance, you encounter yourself in a challenging or unfavorable setting. An issue or setback has occurred. Initially, there is a lack of emotional response. There is also an absence of any assessment or evaluation of the event. The brain is actively engaged in the processing of visual, auditory, and kinesthetic stimuli. And only after that, on the basis of these signals, emotions arise: "This is bad, it upsets me, offends, humiliates, angers, annoys ..." And only after that the conclusions are formed:

"I'm always unlucky, it always happens with me, nobody likes me, I am a loser ..."

As evident from the information provided, the process originates with the reception of signals by the brain. They comprise the initial component in the succession. This implies that the initiative for change must be taken by them. In order to alter the circumstances of the occasion and distance ourselves from the lingering impact of previous adverse encounters, it is imperative that we modify the indicators that have served as the fundamental catalyst for these experiences.

And you are already familiar with the process.

For instance, a previous distressing occurrence has become entrenched in both your conscious and subconscious mind. It influences your actual existence, inhibits your ability to adopt a optimistic outlook, prevents you from savoring life's pleasures, and hampers your belief in fortuitous circumstances. Indeed, it is not possible to substitute a melancholic image with a jubilant one. However, it is possible to disassociate from it within one's mind, diminishing its intensity, decreasing its magnitude, lowering its saturation, and subsequently mitigating its impact on one's own self.

Envision yourself as the director of a cinematic portrayal centered around your personal journey. It is solely within your discretion to determine which events should be retained at the forefront and which ones should be relegated to the periphery. You possess autonomous agency in determining the trajectory and circumstances of your life. At present, we lack individuals who can provide counsel on prioritization and distinguishing between primary and secondary matters. One may consider disregarding the significance of all failures and mistakes and instead focus on the most significant aspects of one's life, namely their accomplishments, strengths, and positive attributes.

What is unnecessary and unbeneficial can be minimized, simplified, and intensified. What attributes to your level of optimism, joy, prosperity, and success is your ability to enhance these images by incorporating generous quantities of brilliance, illumination, vibrancy, and a wider spectrum of colors.

Please regard this as an enjoyable artistic endeavor. You wield absolute authority as the sole controller in this domain, and it solely rests upon your discretion to determine which imagery shall be preserved within the motion picture and which shall be omitted. You have the option to exclude any images from your film that have a negative impact on you.

So, alterations to non-resource states can be made provided that one possesses knowledge of the specific images from which they originate. In the realm of non-resource states, we are faced with various factors that erode our strength. These include but are not limited to, fear, sadness, apathy, depression, despondency, disbelief, anxiety, and confusion. All of these states are engendered by adverse perceptions - specifically, those outward signals that have been construed as unfavorable by your interpretation. Please make an attempt to alter it.

A crucial requirement: the commencement of addressing adverse incidents and phenomena necessitates the adoption of a resourceful state. This will provide you with the requisite infusion of fortitude, enabling you to effortlessly counteract any negativity.

Practical task

Please input any knowledge or information pertaining to available resources.

Recall a particular circumstance from your history that caused distress. There is no need to dwell upon distant memories that evoke feelings of profound sadness or even grief. Consider instances of minor inconveniences or setbacks, such as the recollection of misplacing your umbrella or damaging your cherished attire, arriving tardily to your occupation resulting in reprimand, encountering difficulties during an examination, engaging in disagreements with companions, and related occurrences.

Summon forth the visual representations associated with this particular scenario. If you possess a hazy recollection of them, attempt to envision and reconstruct their image within the realms of your imagination. Ultimately, the significance lies not in the picture itself that you witnessed, but rather in your interpretation and perception of said picture. And it is not entirely congruent with actuality. Gradually, many events appear more prominent and impactful than their true nature, or alternatively, more ominous, intimidating, and somber. Please refrain from attempting to replicate an objective portrayal. Instead, allow your imagination to recreate the scene according to its perception.

Now enhance the brightness and depth of these images to their maximum extent. It is possible to enhance their dimensions, as if drawing them nearer towards oneself.

Now, envision shifting these images further from your proximity. Moving away, they decrease. Now envision a scenario in which the images undergo desaturation and lose their vibrancy. Then envision the scenario wherein their sharpness gradually diminishes, resulting in a gradual blurring effect. Now, the image greatly diminishes in size, becomes unfocused, loses color vibrancy, and becomes scarcely discernible.

Please recall the auditory stimuli that you perceived at that time. To illustrate this point, exemplifying instances include the following vocal expressions. How did they sound? What was the timbre of your voice like? Amplify the mental acuity and intensity of all vocal expressions.

Now imagine that they are becoming quieter, even quieter and completely quiet ... In a manner reminiscent of a gradual decrease in the volume of the radio. And now they are scarcely audible, the words cannot be discerned. You switch off the radio, causing the audible voices to cease.

Subsequently, recall every sensation experienced by the physical form. Maybe you were tense? It is possible that you were occupying a somewhat uncomfortable stance or posture. Perhaps you experienced an accelerated heartbeat or quivering hands, and found yourself afflicted with either a heightened body temperature or a sudden chill? Alternatively, did you perhaps perceive any olfactory sensations or did the flavor of a particular dish evoke memories of that specific situation? Perhaps it is possible that you were grasping an object or had a physical encounter with someone, resulting in the remembrance of these sensations?

Enhance their mental fortitude prior to initiating a subsequent process of gradual debilitation. These emotions diminish in intensity and eventually fade away.

Now envision the entirety of the image as a cohesive entity: diminished, remote, muted, obscured, scarcely discernible, devoid of auditory and tactile stimuli.

It can be observed that the negative emotions linked to this situation have become devoid of their influence. You all have not purportedly erased this situation from your memory; rather, it remains palpable in your minds, albeit its impact has subsided to the point of rendering you impartial and disinterested.

The Juxtaposition Of Incompetence And Expertise

The crux of Neuro-Linguistic Programming lies in addressing a single inquiry. Is it conceivable for an individual to possess both a lack of intelligence and a high level of expertise concurrently? It is believed that NLP has the capacity to discern the essential attributes required to embody both aspects and subsequently merge them harmoniously. "This process consists of three distinct steps:

1) Observe and oversee the behavioral patterns exhibited by esteemed professionals in their respective domains. The manner in which they communicate, the content of their message, and notably, the precise element that distinguishes them as authorities in contrast to individuals lacking similar expertise.

2) Following the identification and isolation of these patterns and the particular 'ingredient' through the use of NLP, an effort is made to imbue them into individuals without extensive expertise, with the aim of enhancing their self-assurance, self-worth, and ultimately instilling in them the conviction that attaining expertise is indeed attainable. This infusion is achieved by methodically and recurrently integrating it into diverse educational methodologies.

3) Similarly to the process of identifying and isolating the "expert ingredients," there is also the observation and isolation of the elements that are less proficient. This approach is undertaken with the intention of modifying and/or substituting them with alternative patterns.

NLP has been referred to as the technology pertaining to the human mind, the examination of accomplishments, and the discipline concerning achievements. The objective of this exercise is to substitute the shortcomings of human performance with favorable outcomes.

This substitution is what will facilitate individual growth. Personal growth serves as a prerequisite for attaining your objectives, be they of a vocational nature or in surmounting an issue that has hitherto remained unresolved by conventional means.

The effectiveness of NLP techniques is apparent through their inclusion in numerous workshops and training sessions aimed at expediting improvements. These techniques offer a condensed timeline for acquiring knowledge that has traditionally required years of trial and error for experts to master.

Deciphering Indications: Non-Verbal Communication Cues In Nlp

Numerous studies have demonstrated the significant impact that non-verbal communication exerts on the overall communication process. NLP acknowledges its own influence and has devised several methodologies with the objective of enhancing communication proficiency. In the realm of NLP Techniques, you will acquire proficiency in methods that enable you to effectively interpret and correspond with the non-verbal expressions of others. This encompasses the alignment of body language, vocal inflection, and ocular motions.

To demonstrate, try this:

Enlist the assistance of an individual to collaborate with you in honing this proficiency. Inform him/her that you will initially align your non-verbal cues with his/hers, and subsequently deliberately deviate from them. It is important to observe that even though the other party possesses knowledge of your intended actions, the outcomes will remain unaltered.

In the context of this exercise, your role will be that of the 'matcher'. Initiate a discourse pertaining to a topic that is mutually captivating to both parties.

In the role of the matcher, one effectively engages in the act of subtly mirroring or replicating the non-verbal cues exhibited by one's partner. Emulate his/her gestures, eye movements, eye contact patterns, vocal modulation, and overall body posture.

After a brief interval, intentionally and conspicuously exhibit a contrasting behavior. Maintain coherence with the subject matter of the discourse, while deliberately employing incongruent nonverbal cues. Disengage visual contact, begin surveying the surroundings, conspicuously adjust your bodily position away from your companion, and articulate with a notably altered manner of speaking and vocal cadence. Notwithstanding these alterations, proceed with the discourse with the utmost adherence to the present format. Purposely exhibit contrasting behavior in a calculated manner towards the other individual.

Result:

The conversation starts well. Both individuals are actively participating in the discussion. Upon initiating a mismatch, a conspicuous shift in the demeanor of your partner becomes evident. He/She will begin to exhibit a decline in conversation skills. Please take note of their concerted effort to reestablish visual contact with you. He/She struggles to maintain attention to your words, eventually leading to cessation of speech.

This outcome will occur consistently each time there is a discrepancy, regardless of the other party's awareness of your actions.

Individuals who find themselves on the receiving end of this incongruity tend to respond with feelings of offense, astonishment, or disregard. They perceive that the individual in question has become disinterested in their personal being and the ongoing discourse. This occurrence is a recurring event, despite the mutual recognition that the dialogue was merely orchestrated. They possess the knowledge that the matcher intentionally misaligned their conduct and nonetheless experienced the emotional reactions. Especially if this occurrence transpires in the realm of reality.

The Significance of Nonverbal Communication

This basic experiment demonstrates the considerable influence of non-verbal cues on a conversation. It constitutes 93% of the outcomes in the process of communication, thereby allocating a mere 7% for verbal expressions. It holds significant influence as it elicits immediate reactions from others, encompassing the realm of emotional responses.

Intuitions

The term "intuition" lacks a precise and all-encompassing definition. One commonly acknowledged fact is that intuition refers to an individual's subconscious reaction towards perceiving and subsequently analyzing non-verbal data. Non-verbal behavior is a manifestation of the internal emotional changes. An individual may conceal their emotions and refrain from expressing their viewpoints, yet their sentiments will invariably manifest themselves through their vocal tones and physical mannerisms. The transfer of visual focus, accompanied by a subtle movement of the shoulders, suffices for the recipient to perceive, assimilate, and respond. Within a brief interval of time, these events transpire and produce an altered outcome of the dialogue.

The correlation between emotions, voice, and body can be attributed to the biochemical and neurophysiological alterations that take place. When an individual experiences a state of relaxation, attraction, irritation, or apprehension, biochemical substances and electrical impulses within the body are triggered. The voice, muscles, and overall physical state are influenced by the neurological and biochemical processes taking place in the brain. Muscular contractions ensue alongside alterations in blood circulation. This aspect eludes our complete and deliberate manipulation, thereby ensuring the consistent manifestation of our non-verbal conduct. In addition to exerting an impact on our physical forms, the electrical charges and chemicals within our bodies also influence the external environment. Alterations occurring within these aspects of our being are perceptible to others. To exemplify, consider the scenario of being in the vicinity of an individual who is experiencing depression. Position yourself directly beside an individual who exhibits signs of sadness, while refraining from actively regulating your own emotional state or outward expressions. Please take note that your personal energy level also experiences a decrease. Position yourself in close proximity to an individual who exudes joy, and before long, you will perceive a noticeable uplift in your own vitality. There is no necessity for deliberate contemplation; nevertheless, your physical being acclimates and accommodates itself to the emanations generated by those in your vicinity.

Emotions are unconsciously manifested in the physical body. The alteration of emotional states results in discernible modifications in the movements of the eyes, legs, and arm that can be perceived aurally or visually. There occurs a transference of tension in both the facial and bodily muscles. Additional bodily transformations that take place encompass:

posture

breathing patterns

skin color

size of the lips

Fluctuations in emotions also lead to alterations in an individual's heart rate. It has the potential to either accelerate or decelerate. The students' pupils expand or constrict in reaction to emotional stimuli. In addition, there is a change in the tempo of verbal communication.

These alterations may exhibit a subtle and almost imperceptible nature, transiently manifesting themselves in fleeting moments. Nevertheless, several of these modifications are readily apparent and possess the capability to endure over an extended period of time. There may also be instances where the conversation is brought to an abrupt halt.

Certain individuals hold the belief that they possess the ability to conceal their emotions proficiently, assuming an inscrutable countenance akin to that of a poker player. Nevertheless, there are invariably minor, inconspicuous alterations that a discerning observer can readily discern and exploit to their disadvantage. The only signals that an individual can conceivably conceal are the overt indicators. An inadvertent release inevitably occurs. In addition, these barely noticeable leaks are also observed by the other individual. This association formed well in advance of the development of verbal communication.

Gradually, this subliminally acquired signal began to penetrate the collective awareness of the individuals. This phenomenon is subsequently regarded as the sensation of intuition.

Individuals who possess an exceptionally refined and cultivated intuition tend to exhibit remarkable proficiency in the realm of interpersonal communication. An effective approach to fostering this growth entails initially cultivating a mindset of embracing diversity and accepting individuals for who they are. Remain receptive to their reactions, responses, and forms of communication. Subsequently, afford careful consideration to their nonverbal cues.

Researching the Application of Natural Language Processing in Non-Verbal Communication

Please endeavor to select a specific area, such as eye movements, voice tonality, or similar aspects. Maintain your commitment for a duration of 1 to 2 weeks. Direct your attention to a specific area and thoroughly examine it. Direct your focus towards the nuanced modifications and be cognizant of your response to them. Refrain from exerting control over your own emotions or responses in relation to these circumstances. Use your inherent, unmonitored reactions as a reference to speculate on how the recipient might have responded to these non-verbal behaviors.

For instance, endeavor to cultivate a methodology to deliberately perceive and comprehend variations in vocal intonation. Engage in conversational exercises over telephonic communication. By doing so, one can direct their focus solely on the auditory aspect and abstain from being diverted by visual cues such as facial expressions, hand gestures, posture, and other forms of non-verbal communication.

During the initial phase of the conversation, specifically within the first 90 seconds, it is crucial to give proper consideration to the tone of one's voice. Please observe and make note of any variations in pitch, the fluctuation in tones, the amplitude, and other related aspects. Upon the expiration of the 90-second timeframe, continue the conversation in its regular manner, disregarding any alterations in vocal inflection.

At the conclusion of each day, make a written record of your observations, recognitions, and realizations. This enhances your NLP sensory acuity, a skill centered around refining one's sensory perception.

With each passing day, one's proficiency in a given activity improves. Through further practice, you will gradually develop the ability to align yourself with the other individual's vocal inflections and nuances, without necessitating any deliberate conscious exertion. Moreover, you will likely experience an increased ability to perceive a wider range of auditory stimuli, including the most nuanced and delicate shifts in pitch and tone. Upon reaching this stage, endeavor to speculate about the factors that contributed to these transformations. If deemed suitable, it may be inquired of the interlocutor at the moment of perceiving the abrupt alteration in demeanor. Inquire as to the factors that influenced their change in mood. This can significantly aid in the assessment of the accuracy of your conjectures. Through further repetition, you will enhance your capacity to formulate a greater number of accurate conjectures. This entails the cultivation of your NLP proficiency in the area of Calibrating.

By augmenting your Sensory Acuity and cultivating the proficiency of Calibrating, you will attain substantial enhancements in your communication prowess. You are fully prepared to enhance your skill set or transition to a different field. Take into consideration the correlation between fluctuations in mood and alterations in respiratory patterns as an illustrative instance. Strive to cultivate your expertise in every domain.

Additional Nlp Strategies For Rethinking Negative Beliefs

In the event that you desire to cultivate greater self-assurance, sharpen your concentration, and cultivate tranquility in various circumstances, or if you aspire to instill positive transformations in your life with the aim of adeptly navigating challenges and consistently guiding your mind towards achieving your objectives, I strongly recommend engaging in the diligent practice of the subsequent neuro-linguistic programming (NLP) methods. These techniques facilitate the reframing of negative beliefs into positive ones, fostering a process of personal advancement and self-improvement.

Anchoring Technique

This particular NLP methodology finds application in various other exercises within the realm of neuro-linguistic programming. It facilitates the assimilation of a specific subconscious response and firmly associates it with an external stimulus. By adopting this approach, each time you undertake practice or involve yourself in that catalyst, you stimulate that reaction and induce your mind to think in that specific trajectory. For instance, should you desire to develop the capacity to maintain a state of tranquility amidst social gatherings, thereby alleviating any apprehension associated with human interaction, you can establish a connection between confidence and serenity by means of an external action, such as gripping your forearm or swiftly snapping your fingers. When engaging in the practice of these gestures, you will experience a sense of confidence and tranquility that will swiftly alleviate any feelings of anxiousness within a matter of minutes.

Likewise, employing this method can yield numerous other constructive alterations in your conduct. Allow me to elucidate the steps for practicing it.

Find a tranquil environment where you can comfortably unwind, and achieve serenity by engaging in a few deliberate deep breaths.

Contemplate the positive transformation or sentiment that you aspire to associate with your consciousness. It could pertain to any area in which you aspire to enhance your skills or experiences, or where you feel a deficiency exists.

Please introspect upon a particular instance in your life during which you encountered the specified emotion, and reflect on the sentiments you harbored during that juncture. An instance that illustrates this is if you seek happiness in order to alleviate feelings of depression, envision a moment from your past when you experienced profound inner joy. This could be a memorable occasion like your high school prom night or any other instance where you experienced an effervescence of happiness within yourself.

Please revisit that particular memory and diligently recollect the experience, focusing on intricate details, within the confines of your mind. Gradually culminate towards that pinnacle of unadulterated bliss, and subsequently savor the exquisite sensation.

Given your profound sense of euphoria, seize the opportunity to rehearse the specific gesture that will serve as a symbolic embodiment of this emotional state. If you desire to establish a firm connection, you may execute the act of snapping your fingers three times consecutively. When you perform the second set of snaps, concentrate on intensifying the sensation of happiness.

Envision the image of a content version of yourself approaching and merging with your being, so profoundly that it becomes fully enveloped within you, allowing you to perceive an inner sense of joy.

Savor this pleasurable sensation for a brief duration before gradually dissipating it from your consciousness through the act of redirecting your thoughts elsewhere.

In the event that your attention is directed towards another recollection, proceed to audibly snap your fingers twice and observe whether a sense of happiness ensues following the second snap. If that is not the case, dedicate sufficient effort to practicing the preceding actions multiple times, and in due course, you will establish a strong association between joy and the snapping action. If, indeed, one experiences a sense of happiness upon executing the action of snapping one's fingers, it can be concluded that a psychological association has been established between that particular gesture and the corresponding emotional state.

If you attempt this action on multiple occasions, you will experience a sense of happiness each time you execute the snapping motion with your fingers.

In order to augment the efficacy of the strategy, endeavor to employ a highly evocative mindset while envisioning the scenario, and allocate a substantial amount of time to honing the technique through repeated practice. Furthermore, engage in consistent practice over the course of several days, and you will observe a substantial improvement in your ability to perform the task proficiently. Utilize this methodology to associate various positive emotions with external stimuli, enabling you to exude confidence, happiness, concentration, attentiveness, and mindfulness at will, regardless of your surroundings.

Furthermore, it is advisable to adopt the visual squash technique as a means to replace any unfavorable behaviors with more constructive ones. By doing so, you can enhance your personal development by acquiring admirable characteristics and virtues, utilizing them to positively shape your future.

Visual Squash Technique

Natural Language Processing (NLP) bestows individuals with the ability to cultivate their cognitive faculties in a manner aligned with their aspirations, thereby facilitating the acquisition of a repertoire of positive behavioral patterns and augmenting the quality of their existence. To enhance your ability to concentrate, engage actively, maintain heightened awareness, demonstrate self-assurance, display a diligent work ethic, and exhibit perseverance, it is recommended that you consider employing the visual squash technique as a means to pursue your desired accomplishments and achieve your targets. It facilitates the amalgamation of disparate propositions, concepts, or even affective states, yielding a novel outcome conducive to attaining the intended objective. For instance, if one has a desire to overcome smoking, it is possible to draw upon a previous instance of disgust and amalgamate it with one's sentiments towards cigarettes, thereby utilizing this amalgamation as a motivating force to cease smoking.

Likewise, you have the capacity to attain any desired outcome and cultivate the ability to establish or modify behaviors, enabling you to effectively pursue any aspirations in life. Let us examine how you can implement it.

Consider any area in which you desire to enhance your skills and capabilities - whether it be the cultivation or abandonment of habits, or the aim to foster positive emotional growth within yourself. Let us proceed with cultivating a sense of aversion towards cigarettes, to the extent that you no longer harbor any desire to partake in smoking.

Please position your left hand in front of you, with the palm facing upwards. Visualize yourself engaging in the act of smoking, and metaphorically hold this imagery within your left hand. This is the current issue at hand.

Generate an elaborate and precise graphic depiction of this issue, encompassing sensory elements that encompass the olfactory, auditory, gustatory, tactile, and visual dimensions of said issue. If engaging in tobacco consumption currently provides you with a sense of gratification, you may consider its attributes such as aromatic presence and pleasant taste.

Please extend your right hand forward and reflect on any source of profound aversion that could be harnessed to augment the act of smoking. One could consider the experience of one's past sickness, specifically the instance of vomiting, and vividly imagine the intricacies of that particular scenario within the confines of one's mind. Envision grasping that photograph within your dexterous palm. This is the state that you have expressed a preference for.

Now proceed to generate a lucid and comprehensive graphical depiction of this particular state as well. This may give rise to displeasing flavors, odors, and textures, among other factors.

Subsequently, engage in a process of sequentially imagining the envisioned and challenging circumstances, systematically alternating between them on multiple occasions. Please perform this action approximately ten times.

Now, please bring your hands into close proximity and apply significant pressure by pressing them firmly against each other. Through this action, you effectively merge the problem and desired states together, causing them to become intertwined and submerged.

Perform this action approximately 5 to 10 instances, thereafter, envision yourself engaging in the act of smoking. If you have effectively employed this methodology, the mere contemplation of grasping a cigarette will elicit profound feelings of repulsion. If not, begin the process anew, commencing from the initial stage, and engage in repeated iterations of the exercise until you are able to achieve the intended outcome.

Subsequently, proceed to gently glide your hands across the preferred area of your physique, allowing the sensation to permeate and establish a profound connection between that specific body part and the emotional state currently experienced. For example, you may apply and gently massage it onto various parts of your body such as the arm, leg, and abdomen.

Now, palpate that region of the anatomy, and it is highly likely that you shall experience a sense of repulsion, as your thoughts gravitate towards cigarettes and even the act of smoking.

Engage in repetitive exercises in order to enhance your proficiency in executing this technique. It can be utilized to enhance a detrimental state and emotional disposition as well. As an illustration, in the event that one tends to frequently engage in procrastination and desires to cultivate a greater sense of enthusiasm towards their work, they may employ a technique wherein they deliberate upon the period of procrastination for a particular task. By associating unpleasant emotions, sensations, tastes, and sounds with this state, they can effectively form a problem state. Subsequently, they can then identify an alternative activity or subject matter that evokes genuine enthusiasm and employ it as their desired state. Evoke positive sensory experiences such as delightful sensations, flavors, sounds, and more. Engage with it and subsequently merge the two states to cultivate a heightened sense of enthusiasm and motivation towards attending to your significant tasks. Utilize this methodology to attain diverse desired outcomes, enabling gradual self-transformation and the realization of one's aspirations in life.

How To Feel Motivated

At this juncture, you possess the capacity to reframe adverse experiences and cognitions, thereby cultivating a more constructive outlook regarding your abilities. Now, it is imperative to transcend mere constructiveness - to attain tremendous success swiftly, you must ensure that you maintain motivation whenever confronted with a task. By cultivating a strong sense of motivation, one can adeptly confront and overcome any challenges with remarkable efficiency, thus enabling a genuine enthusiasm towards accomplishing tasks.

The Swish Pattern

The Swish Pattern constitutes an established neuro-linguistic programming technique that empowers individuals to forge robust correlations fostering favorable conduct, even amidst circumstances evoking ambiguity. This approach has proven highly effective in assisting numerous individuals in managing anxiety, as well as providing them with added motivation to engage in activities they may lack enthusiasm for.

The underlying principle of this technique is straightforward - it facilitates a cognitive process wherein your brain arrives at a subconscious determination that the activity you previously lacked enthusiasm for is now one that elicits excitement. By establishing that connection every time you experience lethargy or demoralization, you will come to recognize your ability to excel in any undertaking through your own steadfastness and dedication.

Regardless of whether you are inexperienced in your role and have not previously performed a specific task, as long as you possess the drive to complete it, you will not be intimidated by your objectives. Additionally, you will discover that a minimal amount of exertion is required on your part in order to effectively demonstrate resourcefulness. By increasing the incentives associated with your goals, you will be motivated to strive for excellence in order to attain them.

The Technique

Outlined below are the sequential measures required to successfully execute the Swish Pattern Technique:

Determine your cue by contemplating the scenario that typically induces feelings of low self-assurance or diminished motivation. This could potentially be the instance wherein you enter the workplace area, only to have an apprehension that your superior will unexpectedly emerge and commence issuing assignments that you perceive as unattainable to complete within the given timeframe. Envision that specific scene with utmost clarity. Envision a scenario where the vibrancy of both the colors and the sounds in that particular scene is heightened.

Please disregard this scene, as if you were gracefully exiting a room, leaving that particular scenario in the past.

Consider conjuring an entirely dissociated mental representation, akin to that of your telephone contact information. Imagine your telephone number prominently displayed in bold font before you, visualizing it clearly. Verbally articulate the numerical values. Subsequently, reverse the order of the digits and read them aloud. As you did previously, please set aside this image.

Now, envision a scenario in your mind's eye where you can perceive an idealized manifestation of your own being. Consider the prospect of attaining a promotion or assuming leadership over an exemplary team within your professional setting, which would subsequently culminate in receiving accolades for the triumphant completion of said project. Perceive yourself as the adept leader that commands the respect and admiration of all. Envision yourself as the individual whom your colleagues aspire to become in the next five years.

Consider that portrayal of yourself as the prospective manifestation of your future self. Enhance your self-perception by expanding the scope and vibrancy of your self-image. Subsequently, contemplate the accompanying emotions evoked by this specific scenario - ponder the resounding clarity of the applause upon receiving commendations, and envisage the tactile sensations associated with the pristine linen shirt draping your person on such an auspicious occasion. If this visual stimulus elicits a positive emotional response within you, then verbalize it audibly. Express your enthusiasm and eagerness to assume this role promptly.

Envision this gratifying visual gradually receding in magnitude, akin to its swift transformation into a minuscule point. Subsequently, restore it to its original life-size dimensions. Continue practicing this technique until your cognition is able to effortlessly broaden the mental representation.

Please take a moment to reflect upon your cue once more, and conjure up the scenario in which you typically experience a lack of confidence or motivation. On this occasion, envision your mental representation of your future self encapsulated within the confines of the aforementioned scenario. Please envision the luminous dot emanating a shimmering glow amidst the ambient surroundings. Now, expeditiously broaden the satisfying scenario to encompass the cue.

Experience the pleasurable sensation that swiftly supplanted your previous emotions as a result of the cue.

With frequent practice of this technique, one will come to recognize their capacity to self-motivate within a brief timeframe of 30 seconds or less, contingent upon the swiftness with which they are able to conjure their cue and envision their triumphant future self. When faced with arduous undertakings or when confronted with adversity, employing this approach consistently will enable you to reassure yourself that you are merely encountering a temporary hindrance. Given your awareness of the pleasant sensation that arises from imminent success, your mind will inherently conjure that mental image in moments of discouragement.

Chapter five - Essential considerations

One of the most formidable facets of overseeing NLP operations involves ensuring coherence and logical progression throughout the implementation phase. There exist numerous methodologies for utilizing NLP; however, one of the most unfavorable approaches involves furnishing individuals with a tool that can be used to criticize or undermine your efforts. Throughout the process of acquiring knowledge, you will become accustomed to the underlying challenges associated with natural language processing (NLP) and the imperative it carries for effectively and unambiguously communicating with individuals.

What is the procedure for accomplishing this? How do you ensure that your proposals and statements conform to the correct format?

The fundamental principle at play here is straightforward: when engaging in conversation, provide the interlocutor with a meaningful contribution that will influence their subsequent reaction. Do you often pose challenging inquiries to individuals which result in them being presented with an insurmountable dilemma? Do not be taken aback by their subsequent expression of anger and exasperation. Assume accountability for your communication style, and you will significantly enhance your chances of achieving success when utilizing NLP techniques, thereby enabling you to effectively modify and shape circumstances for the purpose of improvement.

- Promptly acknowledge that the perceptions of others are not something to be disregarded. The reactions of individuals are influenced by the perspectives and judgments of others. Therefore, it should be anticipated that expressions of disdain, ridicule, or disrespect towards their viewpoints and concepts may elicit angry responses. Each individual harbors their own beliefs regarding the primary concerns in development, and it is imperative to comprehensively grasp one's current perspective prior to engaging in the matter.

- Individuals do not deliberately make poor choices, nor do they engage in such behavior for amusement. Do not succumb to the notion that individuals are intentionally causing failures. We consistently strive to make optimal decisions based on the available information and alternatives afforded to us at any given juncture. It is important to recognize that the majority of individuals are not morally flawed, and thus should not be stigmatized solely on the basis of occasional poor choices they may make. Please endeavor to incorporate this mindset into your interactions with others, bearing in mind that they did not intentionally make any mistakes.

• The truth you are in pursuit of and the truth that others strive for can diverge completely. It is imperative to always bear in mind that each individual possesses their own unique perception of reality, and it is your responsibility to acknowledge and honor this divergence with due regard. One should refrain from making hasty assumptions or judgments about someone's point of view, as it is important to acknowledge and respect the diversity of perspectives. As long as you maintain your personal convictions, it should not be a significant matter.

• Individuals engage with their personalized interpretations of reality, rather than relying on an extensive set of evidence-based options centered around the same perspectives you observe. Views and viewpoints evolve, underscoring the significance of striving to bear this in mind to the greatest extent feasible as one progresses in their life's journey.

These fundamental principles hold profound significance when it comes to apprehending the essence of NLP, which primarily aims at cultivating a diplomatic mindset that actively seeks resolution. By adhering to these courses of action, you will prevent the possibility of limiting your opportunities and, instead, guarantee that you are creating avenues for potential long-term success.

Perceptual Position

Have you ever been able to readily offer advice to others during times of difficulty? Have you ever contemplated the reason behind your ability to dispense advice to them with relative ease? Many individuals possess the ability to offer counsel or remedies to others' issues by virtue of their unique perspectives and insights. What if we encounter challenges without the availability of any guidance or resolution?

Within the realm of natural language processing, there exists a methodology that can be employed to address a given challenge by offering alternative viewpoints. This methodology is recognized as Perceptual Position.

By altering the perspective, it is possible to offer varied evaluations of the identical issue. Through the utilization of this technique, one could evaluate aberrant patterns of behavior or detrimental habits by broadening one's perception or perspectives.

The primary three perceptual positions are:

1. First Person Perspective

By prioritizing our own needs and desires, we can sincerely value what holds significance in our lives. We perceive, perceive auditory signals, and experience the circumstances we encountered through our individual perspectives. Currently, we solely consider the advantages for our own individual interests and deliver evaluations founded upon our own outlooks and interpretations.

We observe, perceive, and experience the situation firsthand, through our own visual, auditory, and sensory faculties. Therefore, we are currently in a state of affiliation with the challenges that are being encountered.

2. Second Person Perspective

In contrast to the perspective held by the first person, our beliefs are inherently influenced by personal experiences, leading us to perceive them as universally true and predisposing us to hastily form conclusions. By adopting the perspective of the second person, that of others, we can ascertain the moral correctness of our actions and words.

We assumed the role of observers, whereby we situated ourselves as 'others' who perceive, listen to, and experience our predicaments.

3. Third Person Perspective

In this role, you will have the opportunity to assess the interaction between the primary and secondary individuals in a disengaged manner. Adopting such a perspective enables one to approach the analysis in a more objective and detached manner, thus facilitating the identification of information that may have eluded the primary and secondary individuals involved.

The role of the third person perspective can also be referred to as an observer or evaluator who assumes an external viewpoint in relation to the first and second persons.

Perceptual Position

1. Choose a situation you want to improve in some way. First and foremost, I would suggest that you begin by selecting a minor issue. As you gain proficiency in employing this approach, you can gradually apply it to more significant problems.

2. Initial step: Commence the thought process by taking into account the

situation from one's own vantage point. You are positioned directly before Mr. X. Observe your eyes, listen through your ears, and empathize with your emotions to gain insight into what Mr. X might communicate to you. Please ensure that you are in the appropriate state.

What happen this time? What are you doing? What actions or statements were made by Mr. X towards you? What are your desires or preferences in this particular circumstance?

3. Break state.

4. Taking on the perspective of Mr. X, let us consider the second position. You are addressed as Mr. X and currently directing your attention towards an individual standing in close proximity. Please reconsider the interaction from the perspective of this individual. Direct your focus towards the reflections and

discernments that emerge while you engage in the act of observing the individual present in the distant vicinity.

What is your desired outcome in this particular situation? How do you perceive your emotions when you witness the manner in which 'You' conduct themselves towards you?

5. Break state.

6. Third position: As an impartial observer, without prior knowledge of the circumstances, please consider the perspectives of both the first party (yourself) and the second party (Mr. X). Revisit the scenario, envisioning it as though you were observing a film. Please take note of the knowledge acquired from this particular viewpoint.

Please observe the circumstances carefully and identify your emotional response upon witnessing their interactions. As a impartial individual, what recommendations can you offer to both parties, drawing from your analyses of their interactions? How can they possibly acquiesce to this proposition?

7. Break state.

8. Revert back to the initial stance. Take note of the alteration in your emotions as a result of your evolving comprehension in association with Mr. X. Pay heed to the recommendations offered by the observer in your proximity. Please be mindful of the discrepancy in your experience. What did you learn? What is the recommended course of action for implementing the suggestion or advice provided by the observer?

If you have not experienced any notable modifications, or should you desire to explore additional alternatives, please proceed with repeating the process from step 4. Every iteration will yield fresh data, perspectives, and knowledge that can be leveraged to tackle the challenges at hand. Concluding with the initial position serves to solidify the modifications implemented in one's future response.

www.ingramcontent.com/pod-product-compliance
Lightning Source LLC
Chambersburg PA
CBHW050244120526
44590CB00016B/2214